SHOUT IT BEAUTIFULLY

BREAKING FREE FROM FEAR AND FINDING MY
VOICE

BONNIE COUCH

POWERFUL
BOOKS

THANK YOU

Sally, thank you for being faithful to listen to God's urging and calling me home. I love you, my friend.

To my children, Amanda, and John. Thank you for letting me have the time of my life being your Mom. Then thank you again and my children-in-love for letting me spoil your children completely. Your love and support during this journey means everything. I love you all.

To Emma Mack. Thank you for putting up with my impatience. I love you. Also, I apologize. I know I wasn't supposed to add to the book after you went through it, but I did. I added some things I was too afraid to add at first. I double and triple check everything. Please forgive me. Did I tell you that I love you?

Perry Power, you are first, last and in the middle. This wouldn't be happening if it weren't for you. You are absolutely amazing. You are loved by us all.

To everyone in the Power Book Community. Thank you for being there all the time. Even at 3 a.m. Oklahoma USA time. I can now say I have precious friends from all over the world.

But most of all, I want to thank my husband, Johnny, for supporting me and loving me for the last forty-seven years while we both healed from years of childhood abuse from our fathers. Thank you for being patient and for all the peanut butter and jelly sandwiches you ate while I was trying to finish this book. I love you forever.

INTRODUCTION

Everyone has a story to tell. I know everyone who has been abused in any way has a story to tell. Whether they choose to tell it is up to that person. I was abused by my father from my earliest memory until I left home and then some more. He used threats to keep me silent about the abuse he inflicted. He proved he was capable of carrying through with his threat by beating all of us severely.

I did not truly start working through and healing from my childhood abuse until my mid 50's. Before that, I was just frantically trying to hide my past and juggling different masks that I had perfected to make it appear that I had my life together. I could be anyone I needed to be. A professional office worker, a stay at home Mom, a successful business owner, a college student. I've been slender, elegant, fat, and frumpy, depending on how my life was going at the time. My make-up and hair had to be perfect no matter what I was doing. I'd have to check it, reapply it, brush it. Whatever it took to keep the look. If I let the mask slip, people would be able to see the real me. The shameful, ugly, dirty, disgusting person I was underneath all my masks. Once I started facing up to my past, started owning my story and shed all my masks, then the real Bonnie slowly started to emerge.

This book is my story. It's real, it's ugly, and it's hard to read. It will have triggers for many. It had triggers for me as I wrote it. It was one thing to have these memories flitting around in my brain. It was completely different to see it written down on paper where it could be read in detail, over and over. My hope is that others who have experienced the same, will know they are not alone, and for those who have been blessed and not experienced any of this, to be made aware of what is happening to children behind closed doors. While my story took place in the 60's and 70's, nothing has changed. The problem still exists. If anything, it is more prevalent.

I hope my story moves you to be more aware of what children are suffering through, and what adult survivors of childhood abuse deal with daily. And if you have a similar story, then I hope you will realize that you are not alone and that there is hope for a life full of joy.

1

FEAR

Fear: to be afraid of someone or something as to be dangerous, painful, or threatening.

THERE ARE four types of fear. Fight, flight, freeze, and fawn. The first three types are pretty much self-explanatory. The fourth type, fawn: to try and please whoever is triggering the fear response to prevent them from causing harm. That's the one that I would become well acquainted with.

I DON'T HAVE a lot of early memories. Just a few, but they're clear memories from when I was three to four years old. I know I was born in Oklahoma City, Oklahoma and we lived in and around that area for the first few years of my life. I've seen pictures of my mom and Dad holding me and smiling like proud parents. I'm always dressed really cute. Blonde hair, blue eyes, chubby cheeks. You know, the cute photo of the two-year-old holding the phone to their ear. Adorable. So from the photos, I am going to say there was a point that they were happy with me. But then I have memories that speak differently.

I'M in a hallway playing with a toy train. My dad comes down the hall, grabs me, and takes me into the living room. He's dressed in a t-shirt and underwear. He grabs me and starts shaking me upside down. Screaming at me. I don't remember what I did wrong if anything for him to be yelling at me. Every few shakes I feel his mouth on me. I remember being upset because he was putting his mouth where I pee. Whatever he was doing hurt. I'm screaming and crying. I see my mom walk in the door in her nurse's uniform. My dad drops me and tells me to get in bed and he starts yelling at my mom. I don't remember anything after that.

ANOTHER FLASH OF MEMORY. Dad and I in his truck going home. I needed to pee. He said to wait until we got home. Evidently I couldn't hold it because I peed on the seat. He was furious. He took me in the bathroom at home, stripped off my clothes and sat me on the counter. He started washing me. He made me spread my legs to clean everything. Then he got on his knees and started licking between my legs. I could see, what I know now, to be his penis in his hands.

I LEARNED at an early age to not make my dad mad and to avoid him. If my mom walked in the house anytime this was going on he would yell and sometimes hit her. He would never let her see him touching me.

. . .

MY CHILDHOOD, I now know, was not anything close to normal. It looked normal from the outside. No one would have ever guessed what was going on inside our house. My mom was a registered nurse. I don't have many memories other than that. I don't remember doing anything with her. It seems that my Dad was around the most. My dad was a talented carpenter. He built beautiful homes and beautiful cabinets. My dad was also an alcoholic.

WE WERE in the den watching TV. Mom yells for us to come to her. I run because she sounds really mad. I find her in the kitchen standing over our father who is slumped over in a chair, passed out drunk. It's the first time I've ever seen him like this. She proceeds to yell about how worthless he is. That we will never be able to count on him for anything. I am so young I don't understand what "drunk" is. She keeps yelling at Dad even though he can't hear a word she says. That's what I remember most about my mom, the yelling.

WE MOVED a lot through my childhood. It's how I can remember events, and my approximate age. The next place I remember living was the little town of Tryon, Ok. My dad was helping build a house for my mom's twin sister. It was located outside of town on a farm. I loved my aunt. She was big, loud, kind of intimidating, and funny. I loved my uncle too. They had two children living at home and other grown children. Our Cousins were a few years older. They were always loud, laughing, and full of life. So different from our home. We were living in this house as it was being finished on the inside. I could see my parents watching TV in the living room. The walls were just studs. I watched my dad get up and tell Mom that he's going to check on us kids. He walks to where we are sleeping. I pretend to be asleep. Hoping if he thought I was sleeping he would leave me alone. He tells Mom that I can't sleep and he is going to lay with me 'til I fall asleep. I freeze. I know what's coming. I'm only five, but this has gone on so long I know what my dad is going to do. I don't understand what my dad is doing, but it's the same every time. He starts rubbing my back, then makes me roll onto my back. He rubs the front of me stopping on my breasts and between my legs. He squeezes my tiny nipples so hard I almost cry out, but don't because I know it will get worse if I do. The entire time he is rubbing himself against me. I stare at the TV and tell myself it will end when this show ends because then my dad's favorite show comes on and he will leave to watch it. I can take it. Just 'til the end of this TV show.

It was September 1964. Dad built a house for us in the same town as my aunt and my mom's mother. He never completely finished it while we lived in it, but at least it had solid walls. I remember the walls because once my dad punched a hole in the kitchen wall while he and Mom were fighting. I had a room to myself and my two brothers shared a room. Sometimes at night I would sneak into my brother's room and crawl into bed with them. If I was not in my room, then my dad could not get to me. I came up with all kinds of ways to avoid my dad. I would eventually get a beating from him, and get told to stay in my own bed at night. I turned six that September and started first grade. It was the first time I had ever been to school. I loved school. It was another escape. I was in trouble a lot because I couldn't sit still. I was almost manic. I spent all day with friends, away from my parents. I was so excited I just couldn't be still. I was taller than everyone else in class. I would be that way most of my life. Some of the kids made fun of me, but I didn't care. I was free for a little while.

. . .

I ALSO HAD my aunt and Grandma close by and I spent as much time as possible with them. My aunt had a tire swing in a tree that was easy to climb. We would play in the barn, swim in the pond. They butchered their own meat and made butter. I loved it there.

WHEN I STAYED with my grandma, I could walk there from our house. We were just a few blocks away. She would fix the foods I loved. She made the best macaroni and cheese. I called them bones because to me the noodles looked like bones. When I spent the night with her she would rock and sing me to sleep even though I was probably too big.   She had a plum tree in the front yard. I still remember the smell of the rotting plums on the ground. There was a huge pear tree and she made a preserve called pear honey with the pears. It was so delicious. 4-o-clocks, a flower with beautiful blooms that opened up around 4pm every afternoon, grew all around her house. The crepe myrtles grew taller than her roof. To me her house was a fairy house. She didn't have indoor plumbing at first. There was a water pump at her sink and a big one outside. I loved trying to pump them for her. And she had an outhouse with a Sears catalog for toilet paper. She always had a bowl of those sugar-covered orange wedge candies. She had an old treadle sewing machine. She would let me push the treadle with my hand to make it go when she had sewing to do. I loved her so much. I hated going home. I would beg my grandma to let me stay. Sometimes she would let me stay longer. But I would eventually have to go home. My first night home, my dad would find a reason to lay in bed with me. Touching me, rubbing me, hurting me. I would cry silently and disappear into a story in my mind. One I would make up about my grandma's fairy house, telling myself it would be over when the story ended.

· · ·

At times we would visit my dad's parents who lived in Wagoner, OK. I loved going there in the summer. My grandpa would always take us fishing. We would get up early while it was still dark and cool and go to the lake and fish. I don't know if I ever caught anything. I'm sure I was a lot of trouble, keeping my line untangled and my hook baited, but I loved it. My grandpa was diabetic and Grandma made him special pies and bought him special jellies. I always wanted to eat some. They tasted awful but they were Grandpa's, so I still wanted some. Grandpa was funny and fun. Grandma loved us but was stern. One time I asked her to teach me to crochet, but it was a Sunday. She said no because she would not work on Sunday. I always felt safe there even if Dad was there. He never touched me when we visited his parents. There may have never been an opportunity for him to.

Sometime during the summer of 1965 we moved to Stillwater, OK. I'm not sure why. I know my mom worked at a hospital there. Not sure where my dad was working. I just knew I wasn't going to be able to see my grandma. I turned seven and I started second grade there. I missed my grandma terribly. My mom's brother offered Dad a job in his transmission repair shop in Fullerton, California. He would have to attend training and he would have to stop drinking. So my dad left for California and we all stayed in Oklahoma until Christmas break. I remember the day my dad left on the train. I hoped he would never come back. But Dad came back at Christmas and moved us all to California. I don't remember the trip but I remember leaving the people I loved. The only protection I ever had.

When we arrived in California, we ended up moving twice again before I finished the second grade. We moved into a rent house right across the street from our school in Buena Vista, CA.. It only took 5 min to walk home. One day when we ran in the door after school we found Dad slamming Mom up against a wall, screaming at her. Our Uncle was out in our garage and I ran out to him screaming for help. Our Uncle ran in and pulled Dad off Mom. He punched Dad in the face. After everyone calmed down and our Uncle went home, Mom left to pick up dinner. While she was gone, Dad beat me for telling our Uncle about Dad beating Mom. I didn't go to school for a few days. What I don't remember is what my mom did when I would get these beatings. I don't remember her taking care of me. I don't remember anything.

WE MOVED AGAIN, into a house in Fullerton, CA the summer before I started the 3rd grade and we stayed here for three years. The longest I had ever stayed anywhere in my life. It was also the most horrifying three years of my life.

WHEN WE FIRST MOVED TO Fullerton, everything seemed different. Mom and Dad both seemed happier. There were lots of kids on our street. Our parents took us to Disneyland, Knotts Berry Farm. It was wonderful. My mom paid more attention to me than she ever had in my life. While Mom and Dad worked through the day, we stayed with my mom's niece. She had two children and she took us to the beach at least two days a week. Days there were wonderful. We loved playing with our Cousins. The neighbors loved my parents. In the evenings and on the weekends Dad was always out in the garage when he was home. He would make rod iron yard lamps, house lamps, chandeliers, even gates. He was so artistically talented. Some-times we would take day trips as a family, to Old Mexico to get the glass and other supplies he needed to make them. Neighbors would buy his work, or he would be helping someone with their car. Others would be asking Mom's advice on health issues. We got a monkey and a dog. My dad was great with animals. It was one of the best summers of my life. Life was good. Until it wasn't.

2

NEVER EVER LET YOUR GUARD DOWN

School started in September and I turned eight. I loved school. I loved my teacher, and I had a few close friends. Saturdays were filled with cartoons and outdoor play. It was a beautiful Saturday. We were all playing in the front yard with neighborhood kids. My mom was at work. I heard my dad calling me. I ran in the house to see what he wanted. Each of my siblings and I had chores we had to do every Saturday morning before we could go out to play. Mine was to clean the bathrooms, do the dishes and clean my room. My dad had me follow him back to his bathroom. He pointed to a spot behind his toilet and said I didn't clean it. I had to clean it before I could go back outside. So I got the cleaner and a rag and cleaned it. He stood and watched me while I cleaned the spot. When I was done he looked at it and said I still missed a spot. Since I missed a spot, he said I was to take off my shirt and clean it again. I froze. No, not this. Not now. I thought it was over. I had let my guard down. From the age of three to the age of seven he had fondled me, touched me, hurt me. I thought he had changed. I started to cry. He slapped me and yelled for me to hurry up. I slowly pulled my shirt over my head. I bent down and cleaned the spot again. When I finished, he said I also missed another spot in a different place and that I now had to take my shorts off. I took my shorts off and cleaned again. This kept up until I was naked. He then said since I did such a bad job that I was to go lay on the bed and do what he told me to. I went into the bedroom and laid on his bed. He took his clothes off and laid on top of me, kissing me and rubbing on me. I was crying the entire time. This was new. He had never gotten completely undressed in front of me before. He was big, and heavy. It hurt. It was making me sick. I could hear the other kids playing outside the bedroom window. That other world where I was happy. Where everything was perfect. Now I knew nothing was perfect. Everything was a lie. When my dad was finished, he said I was to never tell anyone about what he did or he would kill my mom. I had seen him beat her in the past. I knew he could hurt her. But would he kill her? I grabbed my clothes, and went to my room and dressed. I didn't come out the rest of the day, even for dinner.

DAD DID THIS PRETTY REGULARLY. Sometimes he would make me take all my clothes off and lay on the bed, and sometimes he would stop and let me get dressed and go back outside. I never knew what was going to happen. But it was always in the bathroom. Sometimes I would have to dust and my older brother would have to clean the bathrooms. On those Saturdays, I would see Dad call in my older brother. I never talked to my brother about what went on when he was called in the house. I wish I had talked to him and found out what Dad did to him when he was called in. After Mom got home from work, Dad would go out to the garage where he would have a bottle of vodka hidden, and get drunk. Dad was always mean when he wanted a drink, but after he got drunk he was all mushy and sorry and would promise to never drink again. He would want all of us kids to sit with him so he could hug us. Out of fear we would go to him, but I hated for him to touch me. Mom would scream at us and tell us not to go near him. We never knew what we should do. I was so afraid of my dad that I always ended up doing what he asked.

ONE NIGHT I woke and heard Mom and Dad yelling at each other. I got up and peaked out of my bedroom door. I could see my older brother was standing at our parents door listening. Then we heard one of them slam against the bedroom door. I guess they were loud enough for the neighbors to hear because the police came. My dad jerked the bedroom door open and saw my brother and I. We both ran and hid. I ran to my regular hiding place in the backyard behind some large bird of paradise plants. I guess the police or our parents went to check on us kids because they started looking for us. I was afraid to come out because I thought I was in trouble. When it got quiet, I snuck back in my bedroom and got into bed and fell asleep. The next morning our parents acted like nothing had happened. But my mom had bruises on her face and didn't go to work.

OUR FAMILY ATTENDED church while I was growing up. We attended a Free Will Baptist Church when we lived in Fullerton. One Sunday when they gave the invitation, my older brother went forward and several people, including Mom and Dad were on their knees praying for him. He was crying. Well, I had to go check on my brother and see why he was crying. We were pretty protective of each other at the time. When I got down to the front, one of the men there looked at my mom and pointed at me. Then several people converged on me and started praying. They told me if I accepted Jesus as my savior that everything in my life would be perfect and that I would go to heaven when I died. Well, as an eight-year-old, I took this literally. This was it. This was the answer to all my fears and problems. I said yes!

MY DAD hardly ever did anything to us through the week. Sometimes he and Mom would fight. It was always the weekends that were the worst. So I waited anxiously through that first week for the weekend. Waiting to see if my decision to follow Christ would change my life. Saturday dawned bright and beautiful. But nothing changed. Dad was extra angry. During the bathroom "game" he would hit me every time I missed a spot. I was devastated . Evidently, I wasn't loveable or good enough for God to save me.

I FELT like my mom didn't love me or have much to do with me. I felt like my life was for nothing but being my dad's toy. A punching bag. And now I was so awful, God didn't love me or want me. From my earliest memory there was nothing but pain and fear. I would spend the next six years trying to be good enough for God to love me.

I LOVED to read and I would escape in books. Sometimes I would make up stories about my grandmother and her fairy house. In the stories I made up in my head I had a loving family. My mom and Dad loved me and didn't hurt me. In public, you would never know the horror that was happening to me. None of my friends or our neighbors knew what was happening in our house. We looked like an all-American family except for the occasional fight that the neighbors might hear my mom and Dad have. It all fell into a pattern. School through the week. Abuse on the weekend. My stress reliever was food. I put on weight. Kids at school made fun of me. Called me fat. Ugly. Even my dad made fun of my weight. I hoped I would get so ugly he would leave me alone. No such luck. Then, I found I couldn't see the chalkboard at the front of the room. I told the teacher who told my mom. I had to get glasses. I was made fun of for my glasses. Summer came again. It just kept going. I look back now and I can see that I was depressed, afraid, and anxious all the time. In September I started the 4th grade and turned nine. Once again, life got worse.

3

SEX TRAFFICKING

Our family took summer vacations. We always made a trip to Oklahoma to visit family. I treasured these trips. I was able to see my grandma. She was getting older, but she was still the same loving Grandma that I remembered. I hated leaving and would cry most of the way back to California. One year My aunt and her family traveled back with us and we stopped and saw all the sites along the way. The Grand Canyon, Royal Gorge, Four Corners. We had a great time with our cousin. Whenever we were in a family group like that, it was if our parents were not there. At least it felt that way to me. It was a short reprieve. My aunt and her family eventually left to go back home. I prayed for a miracle. Hoping I could go with them, but it never happened.

WHEN THINGS GOT BACK TO "NORMAL" Dad would always be sure to remind me what he expected from me and would come to my room almost every night even with my mom in the next room. I started trying to think of a way of telling my grandma what was happening, hoping she would let me come live with her. Then something happened that let me know that that would never happen.

IT WAS A SATURDAY. I grew to hate Saturday's. We were all playing in the yard with neighbor kids. It was late in the afternoon, getting close to time for Mom to be home. I was feeling relieved because Dad had not called me in the house for anything. Then I heard him call my name. What could he want? Mom will be home anytime now. I walked toward him. He was at the front door. I remember this day in detail. I could feel the cool cement on my bare feet when I walked up to the front door. He told me to get inside. I grabbed the screen door and threw it back and it hit him in the face. This made him mad. He shoved me down the hallway toward his room. When we got to his doorway he told me to lay on his bed. I knew Mom would be there soon, and thought if I stalled he wouldn't have time to do anything to me. So I looked at him and did something I had never done in my nine years of life. I told him no. His face turned red. He was furious. My door to my room was at the corner of his and he picked me up and threw me across my room. I landed in a large doll bed he had made me. I landed on it butt first and it broke. My legs landed over the end and were scraped pretty badly and my arms were bleeding too. He grabbed me and took me into his room, threw me onto his bed and jerked my underwear off. I looked at the bedroom window. The curtains were open enough that I could see the kids running outside. I was afraid they could see in the window. I rose up to say something and to go close the curtains when I felt the worst pain I had ever felt in my life. My dad was raping me. I was screaming and crying. I don't think he used any lubricant, he just rammed into me dry. He was yelling and saying that I would never tell him no again. He tried to kiss me and I turned my head. When I turned my head I could see in their dresser mirror and I saw the reflection of my mom standing at the bedroom door. I turned my head to look at the door and screamed out for her. She was gone. When my dad finished. He told me to get in the bathroom and hurry up and take a bath. He went into his own bathroom. I couldn't walk. I had to crawl. While I was in the bathtub I could hear my mom and Dad fighting. My mom was asking my dad where all the blood on their bed and the floor had come from and how my doll bed got broken. He told her I was jumping on my bed and fell and landed in the doll bed. That the blood was from my injuries. They continued to fight. He ended up beating her badly enough she missed work for a few days. I finished my bath and crawled into bed.

LATER MY MOM came to check on me. She looked at my legs and my arms. I hurt so bad all over. When she finished and I was laying down again, I looked at her and whispered, "Mama, I wasn't really jumping on the bed. That isn't what happened." She then grabbed me by the shoulders and shook me and said, "Yes, you were jumping on the bed." I knew then that my mom would not help me. Maybe I imagined her standing at the doorway. Later that night my dad came into the room. I almost wet the bed when he walked into my room. He sat on the side of my bed. He said if I ever told anyone about what happened he would kill my mom. He said he almost killed her that day but decided not to. He also said I was to never tell him no again. I believed him.

AFTER MY DAD raped me once, it became a regular occurrence . Now he didn't just lay on top of me and rub around. He would now rape me every time.

. . .

MY MOM'S work schedule eventually changed and she was no longer working on Saturdays. This messed up my dad's plans. She also started trying to keep money from Dad so he wouldn't have enough to buy his vodka. He became edgy, cranky, angrier than usual. A few weeks later he told my mom that he wanted to start taking me with him to the shop on the weekend. There was some work he wanted to catch up on and that I could clean my uncle's office and earn some extra money. I was excited to earn the money, but afraid to go somewhere alone with my dad. When we got to the shop there was no work to catch up on. No office cleaning to do. There were just more of my dad's sick games to play. He would force me to have oral sex with him, or just rape me as he did at home. Then on the way home he would stop at a bar. The first time he parked in the back and told me to wait in the truck. I sat in the truck waiting for him to come back. In a few minutes, a man came out and got in the driver's side of the truck. He said my dad sent him out to keep me company. He talked nicely to me and kept trying to get me to sit closer to him. When he reached out and grabbed my arm and tried to pull me closer to him I fought him and opened my door and ran toward the door I saw my dad go in. Before I got to the door my dad came out and grabbed me and told me to get back in the truck and not get out again. The other man got out and had words with my dad. Then my dad went back inside the bar and the other man got back in the truck with me. He didn't talk nice anymore, he just raped me. My dad was selling me to other men for money so he could buy booze without my mom finding out. Sex trafficking. I was always tall for my age and looked older than I was. Looking back at pictures I looked closer to thirteen than almost ten. Did my dad tell the guy that raped me that I was just nine years old? The next time my dad brought me to the bar he parked beside a dumpster where I could not open the passenger side door of the truck and get out. He parked there every time. The smell was sickening. I lost track of the number of men he sent out to rape me. Each time I would escape into a story I made up in my head.

I DID everything I could think of to get out of going with him to the shop. One Saturday I deliberately got so dirty that I couldn't imagine anyone would want to be near me. He was furious. Mom couldn't understand why it mattered. I was just going to get dirtier cleaning the shop office. So Dad took me like I was. When we got to the shop, he made me clean up in the shop bathroom. He had snuck out a clean set of clothes. To punish me he raped me, bent over the sink in the bathroom. When we arrived at the bar, my dad took his usual parking place by the dumpster and went inside. In a few minutes, a man wearing a big silver belt buckle came and got in the truck. He called me sweetie. He unbuckled his belt and told me he wanted me to lick him. I didn't want to and I started crying. I knew better than to refuse, and tried to give him what he wanted. I started gagging and he got mad and pushed me back and decided it would be easier to just rape me instead. I was actually relieved. It was what I was used to. I could just lay there and escape into a story.

I DON'T KNOW how long the bar visits went on. It seemed to go on forever. Through Christmas, into spring and then it was summer again. Then a miracle happened. I started my period. I was nine going on ten. All intercourse stopped. I guess my dad was afraid of me getting pregnant. My mom gave me the sex talk, but she used medical terms I didn't understand. She didn't know that I already had first-hand knowledge of how to have sex. At least she acted like she didn't know. Dad really seemed to hate me now. I could no longer make money for him. He'd yell and hit me often, but the sexual abuse seemed to be over.

There were other changes happening to my body. I started growing hair everywhere. The hair under my arms could be seen in my summer clothes. I would get laughed at and made fun of by other kids. I asked my mom to show me how to shave it. She would always say "not tonight." Eventually I just took a razor and shaved it. Of course the first person to notice was my dad. I don't know how but he made everything he said to me sound sexual. He made me feel dirty all the time.

I'm NOT sure why my dad left my uncle's employment, but the way I found out was when a real estate agent showed up at our house one evening. My parents were selling our house. I was devastated. For the first time ever I had a best friend. She lived just down the street. We told each other everything. Well I didn't tell her everything, but we were close. The summer of 1969 we moved to a town called Rolling Heights, in Los Angeles county. My dad went to work for a hardware store in a town nearby. I guess he was making good money because my mom quit working as a nurse and stayed home. The house was nice with an in-ground swimming pool. Everyone in our new neighborhood loved my parents. My dad could charm anyone. Anyone who had short term dealings with him thought he was a great guy. Things were okay for a while. No sexual abuse, no beatings. But I had learned to never let my guard down again. Dad would start drinking again. He would get drunk, walk to a neighbor's house and visit. Pretty soon everyone knew my dad was a drunk. My favorite escape was still my books, but I also found television to be another great fantasy world.

I STARTED THE SIXTH GRADE, made a few friends, and set into the familiar pattern of avoiding my dad and escaping into books and my favorite TV programs. By the seventh grade, my body seemed to develop into that of an eighteen-year-old. Most girls might be excited about it, but I was devastated. A group of boys would take turns sitting behind me in class. When the teacher wasn't looking they would reach up from behind and poke me in the side of my breast. I started sitting in the very back row where no one could sit behind me.

DURING THIS TIME, my grandma (my mom's Mom) became ill and my mom went back to Oklahoma with her brother to help take care of her. While she was gone my dad's parents came to California to help him take care of the house and kids while he worked. I was so glad they came. I'd missed them. But I was really worried about my grandma. She never recovered. I cried all the way from California to Oklahoma for her funeral. When we arrived at her house, all I wanted to do was lay in her bed. Her room still smelled like her. I hated my parents for moving us away from her where I couldn't be with her. I hated that I didn't get to see her one more time. I hated my life. I hated all the bad things that had happened to me. I hated everything and everyone.

MY DAD'S drinking had messed up the hardware job and he had to look for something else, so while we were in Oklahoma for my grandma's funeral, Dad decided to find carpentry work in Oklahoma. My dad eventually moved to Oklahoma to start working building houses. He moved in with his parents and Grandpa would go and work with him. Dad promised to send money while we stayed in California for school. At some point, he stopped sending money. I remember one evening all we had for dinner was one can of sardines from a Christmas basket and some crackers. They were awful tasting. I didn't want to hurt my mom's feelings and make her feel any worse than she already did, so I told her they were delicious and that I loved them. Not too long after that she filed for food stamps. It wasn't long before we lost our house and had to move in with my mom's brother. In the spring of 1972 we received a call from my dad. They came home from work and found my grandmother, on the floor dead. She had had a stroke sometime through the day while Dad and Grandpa were at work. So we all traveled back to Oklahoma for Grandma's funeral.

AT THE END of the school year 1972, Dad moved us all back to Wagoner, OK where he was living with his Dad. I didn't know anyone. Both Grandmas were gone and Grandpa was too old to go do anything. That summer was the longest summer. I felt lost, and alone. My dad would treat my grandpa terribly when we were around him. He treated all of us terribly. That fall my parents bought a mobile home and placed it on some land near a local lake and we moved out of my grandpa's house. My mom got a job as a school nurse and I started my freshman year of high school. I guess my mom was depressed too because she hardly ever took a shower or fixed herself up. She would go to school with her hair dirty and greasy. I was embarrassed because all the students knew she was my mom. They talked about how mean she was. Dad was still drinking. He would take jobs that took him away from home for weeks at a time. I loved that. I would immediately feel sick when the bus would round the corner and I would see Dad's pickup in the driveway. I knew that there would be fights. He never touched me anymore, but he would come into my bedroom after I was in bed doing homework or reading and sit beside me and just stare. Sometimes he would try to put his hand on my leg. I would immediately jerk away and say that I had to finish my homework, needed Mom, anything to get him to leave my room. I hated him. At that point, I knew that I would never let him touch me again. I would kill myself first. At that point in my life suicide was an ever present option for me.

WE STARTED ATTENDING a local Baptist church. My mom made us attend church wherever we lived. It was part of keeping up appearances. I met and made friends there that I stay in touch with to this day. It was in this church one Sunday morning in Sunday School, my sweet teacher talked about the love of Christ. She explained Jesus Christ to me in a way that I fully understood his love for me. I didn't have to do anything to get his love, I already had it. It was as simple as John 3:16. God didn't punish me with all the bad things that happened to me in my life. All people have a choice to do what they want and that sometimes those choices hurt innocent people. God doesn't cause people to do bad things, you don't cause people to do bad things, people make that choice. God is there to help you through those times. I went forward in church that morning to profess my belief in Christ. My mom was furious. She said I had humiliated her in front of all of her friends. She had already told all her friends that all her children were saved and going to heaven and now I had made her out to be a liar. She said she was going to talk to the preacher and tell him that I was just doing this to get attention. I didn't care what she said. I knew what I knew.

AT SCHOOL I was so socially awkward. I was afraid to speak to anyone for fear I would say something stupid and be laughed at. I was afraid I would walk funny and be laughed at. I was afraid I would dress funny and be laughed at. I was afraid my hair wouldn't be perfect and be laughed at. I would reapply my makeup through the day because it had to always look perfect. You name it. I was afraid of it. Other students would stare at me and I couldn't figure out why. My husband tells me now that it was because I was 5'10", 120 lbs, long blonde hair, blue eyes, big boobs, and long legs. Maybe so, but that's not what I believed at the time. I just knew there was something wrong with me. I had been used by other men. I was dirty. No one would want a girl who had been broken like me. I had zero self-confidence. It didn't help that my parents were still constantly criticizing me. "If you would wash your face the way you should, you wouldn't have acne" "if you would come out of your room and move around some you wouldn't be so fat." Fat? I wore a size 9/10. I was not fat. But they made me believe I was. Fat and ugly. I had never dated and never had a boyfriend. Probably never would.

ONE OF MY close friends had an older brother. Johnny. His name is John, but he will forever be Johnny to me. I saw him at school, at their home when I visited my friend and at church. He was dating someone else at the time. Then one Friday in 1974 when I was a junior in high school and he was a freshman in college, he asked me out after church during fall revival. He had broken up with his girlfriend. Whenever I was around him he was always so nice, so I said yes. But by Sunday morning he was back with his girlfriend. Broke my heart. Skip forward to spring and he asked me out again. This time we stayed together. We dated for exactly a year. During that time, my mother couldn't tell me enough times that I was an embarrassment to her. That people were going to think I was a slut because Johnny and I sat too close together at church or because I was five minutes late getting home from a date. I don't know where I got the courage or the strength to stand up to my mom, but I did it. Johnny was a little bossy but he was kind to me. He actually wanted to be around me. We had talked about getting married after I graduated high school. He was the best thing that had ever happened to me and I was not going to lose him.

WE GOT MARRIED on May 27, 1976, two weeks after I graduated high school. I was seventeen, he was nineteen. My mother had to sign at the courthouse giving her consent for me to get married because I was under age. It cost $500 for our church wedding and that included my dress. My mom complained every evening about the cost. I had my dress made and my attendants made their dresses. I was working at a flower shop after school so my flowers were free. I didn't know how to be any more frugal than that.

4

MY PAST FOLLOWED ME INTO MY FUTURE

I truly believed that when I married and moved out of my parent's home that my problems were over. I was not prepared for the aftermath of nearly eighteen years of abuse. Even though I no longer lived with my parents, I found it hard to let go of their authority. They still had this power over me. My mom felt it was her duty to come into my home and tell me how to clean my pots and pans, even how to do my laundry. I didn't know how to stop her. She informed me that we should come home for Sunday dinner every other Sunday at their house and the other Sunday at Johnny's Mom's house so it would be even. Same for the holidays. If we spent Thanksgiving at the Couch's, then we were to spend Christmas with them. Then the next year it would be switched around. When I was at home it was Dad that was in control. Now my mom was trying to take control of my life. I didn't know how to say no. The one time I had said no to my father had turned out so disastrous that I seemed to be no longer able to say the word. This made my husband furious. He said we would decide where we ate and where we spent the holidays. Of course he never wanted to go to my family's home. He knew nothing of the abuse that had gone on when I lived at home. He just did not like my parents. So there was a constant battle for control of me going on between my husband and my parents. Of course my husband always won. It didn't mean that we didn't fight about it first. I spent the holidays in fear of what was going to happen if we didn't visit my parents. There it was again. Fear. It was never far away. It was my constant companion.

IT SEEMED BOTH my husband and I grew up in dysfunctional homes. My husband had a birth defect. The bone structure in his right leg was not all there and he didn't have a right hip, so his leg did not fully develop. When he was nine, they removed the right food and fixed the stump so he could wear a prosthesis. When he was little, his father would hide him when people would come over because his father didn't want others to know he had an imperfect child. My father-in-law was a poor example of a father and a husband. Johnny's father was very controlling of the people around him. He thought women were second class citizens and treated them just like that and thought Johnny should treat me the same way.

WHILE MY HUSBAND worked and did whatever he wanted to do, I worked and did nothing. I didn't go anywhere unless we were going together. I didn't have any friends I ran around with unless he approved. I didn't get any money to spend unless he gave it to me.

THEN THERE WAS SEX. The only experience I had with sex was horrifying. I kept telling myself that this was different. This was okay. Johnny loved me and would not hurt me.

.   .   .

BUT IN THE beginning all I saw every time we had sex was my dad and his evil face, or the men he sent out to the truck behind the bar. I kept quiet about it. I was afraid that if Johnny knew, then he would leave me. If he left me, I believed the only place I had to go was back to my parents and that I was never going to do. Eventually it got better. But it took decades to become completely comfortable having sex with my husband.

JOHNNY'S MOTHER was the mother-in-law from heaven. I didn't know how to cook so she taught me how. I could cook fun foods like tacos, hamburgers, beanie weenies and mac and cheese, and a few breakfast foods. But nothing like a pot roast, fried chicken or pork chops like Johnny was used to eating. Mom Couch taught me everything. Including how to make her pies. She loved me. She would even stand up to Johnny if she felt he was treating me badly. To this day I tell everyone that Mom Couch loves me more than she loves Johnny. I say it jokingly, but then again.

MY GOAL WAS to never have to live with my parents again. So that meant keeping Johnny. And that meant him never finding out about my past. So that meant I had to keep him happy. I had to do everything perfectly. I had to be perfect. If I was perfect, then my husband would have no reason to leave me. Perfect wife. Perfect housekeeper. Perfect at my job. Perfect. Stress from my husband, my parents, and a massive amount of stress I put on myself. I lived with anxiety and fear.

WE HAD BEEN MARRIED for about three years when we left Wagoner and moved to Stigler, OK where my husband's father lived. His Dad owned a cattle ranch and Johnny partnered with his Dad on some cattle. This was the first time ever that I lived far enough away from my parents to have my own life. Yes they could call, but at that time it was long distance for them to call me and it cost money. They wouldn't spend the money to call very often. This is when I started to change. I started standing up to my husband just a little bit. Claiming some freedom. I still had to be perfect, but some fears were dropping away. Johnny didn't like the changes. In the back of my mind I started thinking, just maybe he wouldn't leave if I stood up to him. But I still didn't do it very often.

MY PARENTS WEREN'T AROUND but now Johnny's Dad was around. Controlling when Johnny could take off, how much money we could get from cattle sales. Johnny had problems standing up to his father also. Johnny had to make an itemized list of what we needed money for and give it to his Dad and then listen to him tell us what we didn't need to have on the list. And then to make things worse, my dad showed up. He had lost yet another job and asked Johnny's Dad for a job on the ranch and my father-in-law gave him one. So once again my parents lived in the same town I did. My dad went to work on my father-in-law's ranch and my husband was his boss. My dad resented my husband being his boss, and let him know that every day. Of course my husband would then have to let my dad know who was the boss. Then my mom would call me and tell me to tell Johnny to let up on my dad. Caught in the middle again. I was programmed from the beginning of time to be afraid to say no to my parents. But I was married and should be supporting my husband. The constant turmoil was making me sick. At that point in my life if all the stress, anxiety and fear just disappeared from my life, my body would have probably gone through withdrawals.

.   .   .

THIS SITUATION DIDN'T LAST a year. They fired my dad. I was sure he would find a job in another town. But he found a job with another local rancher. So they stayed. At about this same time a TV movie came out titled "Something About Amelia." A movie about a father molesting his daughter. Johnny and I were sitting in the living room watching it and I fell apart. I couldn't stop crying. Years of pent up anxiety, worry, fear, and exhaustion came out. I told Johnny about my dad abusing me. He was the first person I had ever told. I didn't tell him everything. I was afraid to tell him about the sex trafficking. I was afraid it would be too much. I didn't tell him about the bathroom game. Some of it I just couldn't say out loud. Now he really hates my mom and Dad. The first words out of his mouth were, "I'll beat the living shit out of him" and he got up to leave. I ran after Johnny and stopped him. I didn't want to see him in jail for beating an old man. Also, if he did beat him, then the entire family would know everything. That could not happen. It took a lot of pleading and crying, but I convinced Johnny to keep my secret.

IT WASN'T long before my dad lost his job in Stigler and my parents moved to Stillwater for work. After that job, they moved to Las Vegas, NV to work. I couldn't have been happier.

5

THE EFFECTS OF THE PAST

I t seemed like once the truth came out about my past, things started slowly changing between my husband and I. This may actually have been our very first steps towards recovery. It still wasn't perfect, but we were working on it. It wasn't long after that that Johnny stood up to his Dad and we moved back to Wagoner. He partnered with a friend hauling hay in the summer and cutting logs for lumber mills in the winter. A few years later, I got pregnant. After eleven years of marriage, we were finally starting a family.

THIS WAS IT. This was my time to be the kind of Mom I never had. My kids were going to be so happy. They were never going to feel fear the way I had to. They were going to feel safe and secure. I would make it happen. From the beginning I had my baby girl dressed to the nines. She always looked adorable. Her room had to be as perfect as it could possibly be. I had professional pictures taken every few months. To me she was the most beautiful little girl I had ever seen. I took three months off from work when she was born. I treasured every Moment. Most of her naps were taken laying right on my chest. I had a carrier so she was carried right up against me while I was doing chores around the house, or shopping. She was next to me most of the time. When I had to go back to work, I would get up extra early to have time to rock and sing to her before I left. When I got home from work, I made sure to take my time feeding her, bathing her, talking, and singing to her. I never just laid her down in bed to sleep. We always rocked and sang her to sleep. Sometimes it was her Daddy who put her to sleep. This child would know she was loved. It was almost as if I was recreating the fairy-tale stories that I disappeared into when my dad was abusing me. When our daughter was three months old, Johnny bought and started driving a truck. He was never gone overnight. Sometimes his days were long, but he was home every night. I was working in the accounting department of a manufacturing plant. Johnny always stressed over money. If he thought I spent too much on groceries, he'd yell. If the electric bill was too high, he'd yell. If anything was too much or prices were too high, he'd yell. I'd always take it personally and feel like it was my fault, like he was blaming me. So I got to where I wouldn't tell him the entire amount of the grocery bill. I would tell him our daughter's clothes came to twenty five dollars instead of fifty. Sometimes I would charge things on credit cards and not tell him about it and try to pay the card payment without him knowing it. Anything to keep from getting in trouble for the cost of things. I never could pay the credit cards off completely. The balances would keep getting higher. I would pay the minimums and just bury my head in the sand.

THREE YEARS LATER, we had a little boy. He was perfect. Our family was perfect. We had a boy and a girl. I was able to take six months off work after I had him. I did the same with our son as I did with our daughter. I dressed him like a little cowboy. Just like his Dad. I did my best to create a safe world around my son. I worked to make their life as perfect as possible. I wanted their Christmas to be big and exciting. I wanted their birthdays to be extra special. Johnny didn't think that was necessary and didn't want to spend as much money. But I wanted it to be perfect. I would have lights all over the outside of the house at Christmas. The inside had a tree in every room. What I didn't realize at the time, was I was doing all of this to make up for not being enough. I was still dirty, ashamed, broken. I had to have everything perfect to make up for being an imperfect person. An imperfect mother. An imperfect wife. But even with all the stress I was putting on myself, I loved being a Mom. My children brought so much meaning and joy to my life.

I WAS DOWNSIZED from my job and decided I would stay home with my two children when my daughter was five and my son was two. The anxiety of someone else taking care of my children was taking its toll on me. We still needed a second income, so I opened a day-care in my home. I worked at that job for sixteen years. It was the most rewarding thing I have ever done. I was able to be with my children as they grew up, while being around other little ones . I had always wanted to be a teacher, this was about as close as I would ever get. But our financial problems were still a problem. We went to counseling and tried to deal with the problem we had about finances. He tried staying calmer about the cost of things. I tried to not hide things from him. But the fear inside my head always won. My head told me I was responsible for keeping Johnny and our children happy so I would be worthy of them, just like I was responsible for keeping my dad happy so I wouldn't get hurt as often.

.   .   .

MY PARENTS WERE STILL AROUND, but I saw them as little as possible. They had moved back to Oklahoma about the time our daughter was born. I still struggled with boundaries. I didn't want My dad to have any chance of hurting my children. My children never had a very close relationship with my parents. The only reason I maintained a semblance of a relationship with them was, if I didn't, I would have to say why. Then I would have to tell the family about what Dad did to me.

JOHNNY and I both grew up in church, but after we got married and had our own home, we stopped attending. At the time it didn't bother me. One reason was, my mom was at the same church we attended, another reason was I was so angry at God that I had no desire to go and worship him. At that time in our life we did things and made decisions that we would regret for the rest of our lives. After having our children we both started feeling differently. When we first started attending church again, we attended the church where we were married. We didn't feel like this was the right place for us and started attending another church at one of the many lake communities around Wagoner. We stayed there for many years. We eventually became Directors of the Children's Department. I loved it. The children were sweet and some were from very low income families, some were just in need of love. Our children were in the age group, so I could keep an eye on my own kids at the same time.

WE TOOK summer vacations in Ouray, Colorado. We would haul our jeep out and drive the mountain trails. It was beautiful. On one trip, we were returning to our hotel room for the day and my husband turned to me and said "I think it's a great idea to bring some of the children from church for one of our vacations. " I looked at him and said "what are you talking about? I thought about that while we were up at the top, but I never said anything." We just sat there and stared at each other and got goosebumps. God was working on both of us at the same time. So in twelve months we had purchased another Jeep, and had four kids, 5th-6th graders picked out to go. Some had never been out of the State of Oklahoma. The next year we were asked by the Pastor of a local Ouray, Colorado, church to help with their summer vacation Bible school. So we purchased another Jeep. We hauled out three jeeps, two high schoolers and eight, 6th graders and helped with Bible school in the morning and took our group on Jeep trails in the afternoon. One of them was really clingy to me. She was by my side at every turn. Eventually she opened up about her home life. She had stories from her home that were heartbreaking. Some of the same things I had experienced myself. I realized right then that God had placed me at that place and that moment to comfort and help that child. The horror that I had experienced would help me relate to children living through the same abuse I did. I almost broke right in front of her. Right there, something good was coming from my awful childhood. Maybe I was going to be okay.

In 2008, my dad passed away. I felt nothing at first. At his funeral, so many nice things were said about him. That's when the anger started. My siblings and other relatives were all talking and sharing good memories and happy times they had with my dad. I had nothing. Nothing good that I wanted to share. I just wanted to scream. Right after that my mom's health started to deteriorate. She went into the hospital and then straight into a nursing home. One day when she was in the hospital, I headed up to see her. I called her as I was headed there to see if she wanted me to bring her anything special. She said yes, bring me some Benadryl. I told her I would just ask at the nurses station if she could have some. My mom said no, they won't get it, just bring some with you. I told her I couldn't unless the nurse or doctor said she could have it. This made her mad and she said, "I knew this would happen after your Dad died. You only did things for us so your Dad would sleep with you." I was shocked. I pulled over to the side of the road and stopped. I couldn't talk or move. I just sat there with the phone to my ear. After a minute of just sitting there numb, with my mom's voice yelling at me in the background, I ended the call and cried. She knew all along, and did nothing to save me from the monster that terrorized me my entire life. I didn't go see her that day. I never went to see her again. She passed away about a year later. I did go to her funeral. The minister talked about how she loved to help out in the church nursery with the babies and the toddlers. And how much she loved the children in the church and all her grandchildren. And I wondered why she couldn't love me. Why wouldn't she save me from the hell I lived through?

A FEW YEARS after my parents died my older brother passed away. He died alone. He was found in his apartment several days after he passed. He was an alcoholic and fought demons of his own. I wish I had had the courage to ask him if Dad had abused him like he had me. Maybe we could have helped each other.

AFTER SEVERAL YEARS we moved to a church in town closer to where we lived. My husband became an ordained minister here and the youth pastor. When he was first asked to be youth pastor, we both said no. Both our children were grown, married. We had raised two teenagers and didn't want to deal with anymore. But Johnny relented and is still Youth Pastor there today.

A PERSON WOULD THINK that I would be able to let all my past go and go on with a happy life since both of my abusive parents were dead. They would be wrong. It was all still there. As big as ever. The fear, the anxiety still plagued me as if my parents had moved in next door instead of being buried. All of my past and the effect it had on my life came to a head one winter's day in 2012. After thirty-two years of trying to be perfect at everything, hiding the spending, hiding my shame, everyone was going to know about it. Johnny found out about a late credit card payment when they called his cell phone instead of mine. They weren't even supposed to have his number on file. As soon as he hung up, he looked at me and said "That's it, we're done." If he really meant it, then everyone would find out everything about my past. People would want to know why we split up and then they would find out how screwed up I was. My entire family would be ashamed of me. They would all be better off with me gone. Our kids would want to know why I put their Dad through all the things I did. It wouldn't matter that he yelled about the money and scared me to death. Johnny would make it sound like he hadn't done anything. That none of it was his fault. So I got in my car with a bottle of pills and left. I just drove. No destination in mind. I was just going to find a spot and swallow the entire bottle of pills. This insane house of horrors had gone on since my first memory at three years old . Fifty years of abuse, fear, anxiety, shame, pain, and trying to keep it all hidden. I just wanted it to stop.

WITHIN THE HOUR of me leaving, my family was looking for me. Everyone started calling and leaving voicemails. I wouldn't answer the calls or listen to the messages. I knew what they would say, and I didn't believe them. I found a place to stop that had a pretty view and pulled over. All I wanted at that moment was my grandma to rock and hold me and for the pain, guilt, fear, and memories of my past to stop. My phone was constantly buzzing. I happened to look down at one point and saw that it was a close friend from church. I don't know why but I answered. She just softly told me that I needed to come home. That my family needed me and that she needed me. God was using her, because at that very moment something clicked inside my heart and I knew right then that I would be going home. I didn't want to die. I started my car and I headed home. I turned my radio on to my favorite station and a song I had not heard before played. It had to have been written just for me. For that very moment in time. It touched me to my very soul.

'Cause I'm Worn
By Tenth Avenue North

I'm tired I'm worn
My heart is heavy
From the work it takes to keep on breathing

I've made mistakes
I've let my hope fail
My soul feels crushed
By the weight of this world
But I know that you can give me rest
So I cry out with all that I have left

Let me see redemption win
Let me know the struggle ends
That you can mend a heart that's frail and torn

I wanna know a song can rise
From the ashes of a broken life
And all that's dead inside can be reborn
'Cause I'm worn

I know I need to lift my eyes up
But I'm too weak
Life just won't let up
And I know that you can give me rest
So I cry out with all that I have left

Let me see redemption win
Let me know the struggle ends
That you can mend a heart that's frail and torn

I wanna know a song can rise

From the ashes of a broken life
And all that's dead inside can be reborn
'Cause I'm worn

My prayers are wearing thin
Yeah, I'm worn
Even before the day begins
Yeah, I'm worn
I've lost my will to fight
I'm worn
So, heaven come and flood my eyes

Let me see redemption win
Let me know the struggle ends
That you can mend a heart that's frail and torn

I wanna know a song can rise
From the ashes of a broken life
And all that's dead inside can be reborn

'Cause I'm worn
Though I'm worn
Yeah, I'm worn

6

TAKING BACK AND GIVING BACK

I t's been eleven years since the day I thought I would end my life. When I got home that day I made a promise to myself to never again make suicide an option.

I WAS ALREADY IN COUNSELING, but started being more honest about what had happened to me and what parts of my behavior I needed to take responsibility for. Johnny went to counseling also. Sometimes we went alone and sometimes together. But we went. And we stayed the course. I wanted to be free of the guilt, anger, anxiety, and fear. Fear. It's always there. Johnny needed to let go of all the things his Dad had him believing about himself from an early age. His father had told him so many times that Johnny would never be able to support a wife and family. That he would have to live off the government. That he would never be able to get a regular job and earn enough money. So money was a very touchy subject for Johnny. He liked having a lot of money in the bank, and he didn't like spending it. Even on things that we needed. Money in the bank meant his father was wrong and he was capable of supporting a family. If money got too tight, then maybe his Dad was right and he wasn't doing a good job.

I NEEDED to work on my self-confidence, and fear of everything, I needed to realize I was worthy of being loved just as I was, without jumping through hoops. I didn't have to be perfect. As I dug deep into my past, I started having night terrors. It was terrifying. After one exceptionally bad one Johnny found me in the back of our closet curled up crying. My therapist said it would help to remove anything from sight that was a trigger. So I went through my home and removed everything that triggered thoughts, memories of my parents. My dad had made me a lot of wood crafts. I sold them, replaced them, or gave them away. Every time an item left the house, I would have a panic attack. Was I going to be in trouble for getting rid of the item? Was I an awful person for doing it? Why did I have them in the first place? I found, as time passed, that I did not miss the items. I was glad they were gone.

WE TOOK the word divorce out of our vocabulary. Yes, there have been times one or both of us have wanted to just walk out. Sometimes it seemed like it would be easier to live alone. But we didn't. We would pray before we sat down to pay the bills. If I felt like he was getting too aggressive I would try to say something. Sometimes it worked, sometimes we fought. But we kept working at it. I had to change counselors three times. My first one left their private practice, second one retired, and third one didn't accept my new insurance when it changed. I'm on my fourth and she is retiring at the end of the summer. Each of my counselors brought something different to the table. They each had a different way for me to deal with my anxiety, night terrors and fear. I have used all of them. I have had to rewire my brain.

Teach it to react differently to everyday situations. I will find a fifth counselor when my current one retires in August. We will forever be a work in progress. But we will be together forever.

AS YEARS WENT BY, I grew stronger and Johnny grew kinder, softer. Yes, I said years. The harm that this abuse causes does not happen overnight. The healing does not happen overnight either. It took a lot of hard work but life became a little easier. The fears chipped away a little at a time. Triggers do still turn up when and where I least expect them. Smell seems to be the strongest trigger for me. For this reason I will always be in counseling . I want to be strong enough to be ready when the triggers show up. Yelling is another trigger. Today you will find that Johnny and I rarely raise our voices in anger, especially at each other. I said rarely, not never.

I HAVE FORGIVEN MY PARENTS. I was so tired of hating. I don't know what was wrong with them. It's possible they were abused as children. I don't know. I know my dad was abusive to my mom. Forgiveness is key. Forgiveness for yourself and forgiveness for the ones who hurt you. You will probably never get an apology from your abuser. I know I never will because both my abusers are dead. That's okay. Forgive them anyway. Forgiveness is for you, not your abuser. It's a positive step in the process of letting the past stay in the past and living in your future. You can live a life that is happy and free of guilt, fear, and shame. It takes work. I get up every day and remind myself that I am a child of the most high God. That I have the saving grace of my Lord and Savior Jesus Christ. That I am loved by my family and friends. That I am valuable. That my parents were the monsters, not me. I am overcoming the awful things they did to me and am living a life full of joy.

.   .   .

TELLING my story is part of my healing. The first time I shared my story was several years ago with our youth group at summer camp. I told a very short version of it and left out a lot. I don't know what I expected their reaction. to be. What I didn't expect was for them to get up from their chairs, hit walls, walk out of the room, walk up to me crying and hug me. It was very emotional. I loved all of them and they all said they loved my husband and me but that night I saw it. They were angry about what had happened to me. Not one of them looked at me with disgust or disdain. Sharing your story is nothing like you have ever imagined. There was no judgment, only an outpouring of love. The next time I shared my story was recently with my women's Bible study group. I was so overwhelmed with the outpouring of love and encouragement from every woman in the room. Some have even shared their own similar story with me. It was so liberating. If you can reach deep down and find the courage inside of yourself to, just once, share your story, you will not stop at that one time.

I HAVE a voice and I have important things to say. People will listen to me. I can help others who are just like me. I get excited now when I get the chance to share my story with someone and can tell them that they too can find a life of joy after being abused. Life can be good. I did not get to be a carefree child during my childhood. Now that I'm taking back my life, I plan to be a child at heart the rest of my days. My goal is to tell as many people as I can as long as I am breathing that they should never let the monsters of their past, own the rest of their life too. Own your story and own the rest of your life. Take back the joy that was stolen from you.

.   .   .

THERE ARE people in this world that are wretched and merciless. They will hurt you physically, sexually, mentally and rip your soul right out of you. You have to decide if you are going to let the memories of that evil person continue to take the rest of your days until the end of your life away from you, or if you are going to take those days and fill them with joy. Share your story, help yourself and others heal.

7

FINAL THOUGHTS

I have always had a love for children. I think God gave me an extra strong dose of it.

WHILE TRYING TO HEAL, one of the exercises was to reach out to our inner child. To talk to the abused little girl inside. At first I couldn't do it. When I looked her in the eyes I saw wisdom beyond her years, and a strength that no child should ever have to possess. She seemed so much stronger than I was at that moment. I felt ashamed. Then I came to my senses and realized that that little girl was me. I possessed the strength I was seeing in her eyes. That wisdom was mine. I have that wisdom to use and to share. And I am going to use it.

I WANT to reach out to all children and educate them about protecting themselves against predators. We, as parents and family members, should be doing this. Sometimes the predators are the parents or family members. So education should come from all areas. Home and school. There should be a way to work this into the school format. I know there are books about good touch and bad touch, but do they prepare them for the lies that the predator will tell them? The fear it will instill in them? "If you tell anyone about this I will kill your mother." "No one will want anything to do with you if they find out you did this." "You aren't any good, you deserved this." The children will believe these things. I believed these lies when told to me by my dad. Children need to know that they will be told this and to not believe the lies. They need to know to tell someone immediately. If nothing gets done, then tell someone else. To keep telling someone until someone believes them. It's sad, but we have to teach them to fight for themselves until they can find someone to fight for them.

BE diligent and pay attention to your child. Watch for unusual behavior. Ask questions. I would have given anything to have someone notice me and to have reached out to help me. If you think no one wants to talk about this subject today, well in the 1960's as far as people were concerned the problem just didn't exist.

IN A WORLD where you can get on social media and talk about anything and everything, why is the subject of child sexual abuse still being avoided? I know how hard it is to be brave and tell your story. But the more of us survivors who make our voices heard, the more people who are just like us, we can reach out to and help. We can speak for the children who are afraid to speak for themselves.

.   .   .

IF you truly want to speak out, to shout your story, reach out to contact@Iamperrypower. Perry Power has a program to help anyone wanting to tell their story. He is on FaceBook every day, asking for survivors who are interested in sharing their story. Reach out to him and he will show you how you can do it.

MY JOURNEY WAS NOT PRETTY, but I think it has a happy ending. No matter what your past looks like, free yourself and make your future beautiful.

LOVE TO ALL,
    Bonnie Couch.
    #don'tjustcryforthechildren
    #dosomething

Printed in Great Britain
by Amazon